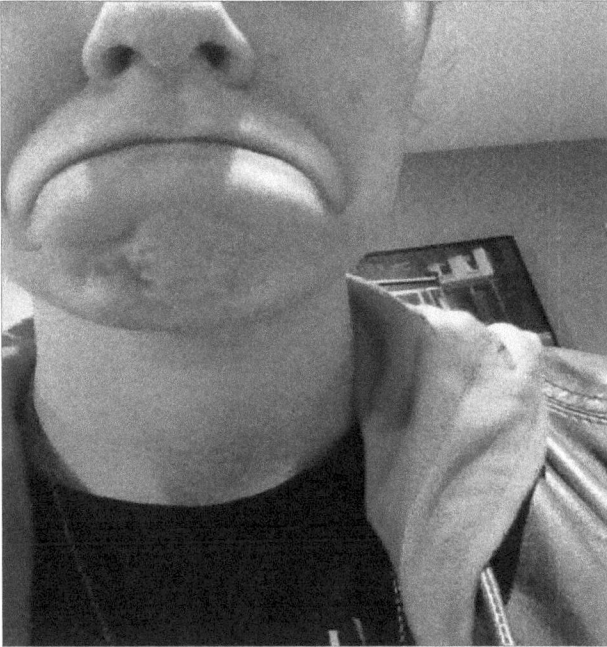

ISBN-13: 978-0615969428 (Natalie Coll)

ISBN-10: 0615969429

Contents

- Frank

In a Circle

- Above the Trees

- Summer

- Vomit

- R-

- Moose

- Moose Knuckle

- Wooah

- Happens

- Kicker

In a World

- Tommy

- Bartholomew

- Nosferatu Pt. 1

- Nosferatu Pt. 2

- Nosferatu Pt. 3

- Agh

- 2010 - An Epic

- Old Man

It's been a few years since my heart passed.

I hope to apologize to those who've killed

me.

I hope to apologize to those who have

revived me.

I hope to apologize and I hope to thank.

It's been killer.

Should a Professor

Continue that Thought

Amp-

Why'd you do this to me?

I'm overcome in poverty

I have gold and lace in my eye

It's hard to believe that you are anyone else

There are spaces in my talk

Can you hear me while I'm standing here?

I can promise that my minds skips

It's hard to believe that I couldn't be anyone

else

Can you tell me which way is home

I've gone off travelling

You don't know where your interests lie

It's hard to believe that we just couldn't be

JW-

Blue is a time for us

When there is no place for us

She likes to sing when there is no width

Then stray away from us

I can't say it's all her fault

I can't say we didn't all want her to talk

She likes to stand inside the building

With eyes in front of us

Samu-

Man, man, oh, man

Look at what's become of you

Point around;

Specifically at the whites of our eyes

Describing the world and its size

<u>Sam-Samu-</u>

Go, time, time, go

Tell me the green is not clean

Tell me my mother is mean

Tell me I've broken the seam

I look around

Though, time is high

My eyes are light

Because it's the lifeline of my sight

I can't hang on to this long, my friend

It's simple as it passed away, and come

along what it may

It's tested again

It's simple and scornful offend

Red Edwards

There came a day when my heart passed

I picked up my bland mission

I picked up a street incision

We tinted dark the car's glass

But when she first came around

And she had undressed her sleeve

We'd found it hard to believe

That she could never be found

That she had ever frowned

-JP

Come on boy, kick your can and

Keep it way above that curly head

Keep it inside the pages and

In those burgundy pants, so fine

I want to seem like it's fine out here

Don't shake and don't move

Like people

Like sculpture

Come on boy, teach me something

Cape your wares, keep your cool

Keep it erotic in my coup de formal

Frank

He was a man who hollered loud

A real teenager if you ask me

A lot larger than anyone could see

Who wore his sash and crown of gold proud

He had a talented mind

He sang a city afloat

He wore a lyrical coat

He had a trick that's worth the find

And when I flew to his mouth

He didn't see me in my frown

He didn't see me look down

So I flew back to the south

In a Circle

Above the Trees

Missing confirmation, what about it

I've walked for blocks

I've walked on the highway

Searching diligently, in the sky

My mistake

It came down for me, another country

Inside the ship

They cut me sideways, scooped my eye

My mistake

It came down for me, threw a party

They sewed me up

They threw me down

They gave me leeway, engraved the walls

My mistake

Summer

My friend fell in the ocean; she was
swallowed by the sea

She had tried hard to be lazy; she had tried

hard to be me

So I waited until the day that she drifted to
the shore

I was trying hard to find her until I couldn't
find no more

I tried hard not to care, but I was feeling
kind of down

So I tried to find the king so I could please
borrow his crown

But when I brought her up from hell,
everyone started to cry

I was casting miracles and when they asked,

I said I'd try

So I tried to find the king so I could give

him back his crown

And try to find a way again to make my best

friend drown

So we drove up to a cliff and I jumped out

of the car

But when she started screaming, she already

was too far

And when she hit the water, everyone had

just dropped dead

And so continued life, at least the one that I

had led

Vomit

Why did you do this to me?

Go away, I'm still here

Can't you see I'm green?

You should have died like all my other peers

So, hello

Can you come here right now?

No, I can't, I'm vomiting

There's a blood stain on my pants

I should have left like everyone else

So, hello

Can you tell me where you went?

I don't know, I can't see

There's a green sign to my left

I should have never followed you home

So, hello

R-

They don't see, they don't see

Now you're here

That they're there, that they're there

That they're there, that they're there

You can see, you can see

That you're there

They don't care, they don't care

They don't care, they don't care

Moose

She had died in aisle nine and I couldn't

stand her up

The Devil sighed with Jesus Christ

As they sat in the back of the line

And no one can know just how far she

would go

To get her prescription filled

On holiday, so far away

I was living in a house of cards

And I don't know if I've been here before

But I know that I'm still lying in bed

Moose Knuckle

It's a beauty outside

It's a day to go to work

Someone chewed on my car tires

Now I'm stuck in the dirt

I'll swallow kerosene

And I'll glow in the night

It's way too black outside

So, I'll ask Black Francis for light

<u>Wooah</u>

I don't know, I can not go

Don't know no more than what I sold

I am a dangerous invader

I sold my car

I think I'm good, a duplicator

Sell my stuff on times new island

Sell my wares

Sell my new white sand

Going, going, just keep going

I am still

I am stop motion

Past is past and I'm still doing

What is good and I'm not going

Happens

Nothing happens all at once

There's only the she, and the they

They don't matter

But she has a dog

And it barks and it's annoying

And it's embarrassing, so we move away

It's barking and we're moving and it's

barking at us

And we continue to walk and it's pulling on
its leash

This poem says and seventeen times

And it only has four characters

And that dog is still barking and she's on the
phone

The table falls over and there's coffee
everywhere

And now it's really barking, if it wasn't
before

And this is happening five more times

And so nothing is happening

And it's happening all at once

Kicker

I know that, you're rich, holy clothes

I know that you're family in your mind

It's fine and

I hear that you're in it

I hear; I hear that you're gold

And everything

I might be interested

If it's strange, if it's right, if it's simple in
the light

You're a posh top machine

With a posh selfless gleam

If it's strange, if it's right, if it's simple in
the light

Then I don't know what it means

I don't know what it means

In a World

Tommy

There is a whisper from the window

In the night inside my home

And I think about my happiness

And all the good that I have done

Inside had crept a small boy

Who had said that Tommy was his name

He said he was my brother

Because we look and sound the same

But I do believe he's wrong

Because in simple song and light

Should something like this happen

Then surely, I am right

He talked so sweet and thoroughly

But I don't know what he said

In the time it took to say his name

He'd shot a bullet through my head

Bartholomew

He swore he was a simple man

That Tommy was his name

Little Barry was oblivious

To the cold December rain

He thought of every picture

That Tommy had ever seen

He had never met the boy before

But he believed he'd always been

Barry was always off-put

Something always happened in his head

If Tommy was no longer breathing

Then surely, Barry would be dead

Nosferatu Pt. 1

Nosferatu came along not too long ago and

we talked a day away

With a gun slung to his side, yellow in hue

He came hollering at me

He came hollering at me about his gun and
his brother

Nosferatu had a brother named Jesus and the
guys gun was blue

He came hollering about his gun and some
words on a page

I said,

"yeah, man"

And let him talk for days

Nosferatu Pt. 2

With a gun slung to his side, yellow in hue

Now, he has another, he's got a blue one out

in the parking lot that he'll pick up on

                    his way

He bought me a drink and made my bed

Everyone was screaming so we stuck our

tongues out the door and he dual wielded

his

weap

ons at

the

speed

of the

next

day

At the speed of the next day, he came

hollering at me about a shot

A shot in the gut, my friend, a shot to the gut

His blue and yellow guns show him down

and that was the last red I saw that day

Nosferatu Pt. 3

Nosferatu came by just the other day and

talked a life away

With a gun slung to his side, yellow in hue

He came hollering at me

He came hollering at me about another that

he's got down in the parking lot

A blue one that he's got that he'll grab on

his way out

He bought me a drink and made my bed

Everyone was screaming so we stuck our

tongues out the door and he dual wielded

                                    his

weapons at the speed of the next day

At the speed of the next day, he came

hollering at me again

Hollering about a shot

A shot in the gut, my friend, a shot in the gut

His blue and yellow guns shot him down

and it was the last red I saw that day

<u>Agh</u>

I'm amazed, guns on a walk

I'm a tame shot in the gut

I told my lover that I'm much too posh

To be a building jumper

I'm amazed -

I've tamed my torn off arms

I swear I know, I am, I'm good, I know it

I'm a ceiling cruncher

I'm amazed, and I told my mom

I'm a tame sinner by sun

I said goodnight and swept that look off my
face

Since I'm a skydiver

2010 - An Epic

It's already been four hours and my name is still only Pre-Warned and I'm still waiting on that guy we interviewed last week.

I think his name started with a J; Jeff, John, Joey, they're all my food stamp and they're taking a really long time.

John comes in and he's sees the time.

No questions asked as he takes the slip from my hand, as well as my debit card, over the register, because cameras do still have eyes.

"It's 2010, remember it," he nods and slips away, scratching the numbers into the receipt slip with his thumb, in case he forgets.

My name is still only Pre-Warned and I still can't remember his.

He's gone and the customer who scooted to his line scoots back and waits his turn, but buys only one thing.

All I can think about is hunger and how Jeff has my time in one hand, my card and my order from the same place at generally the same time in the other.

I never pack a lunch, so sometimes I'm named Forgetful, but there are days I bring extra and leave some in the fridge for the others.

Those days, I'm named Selfless.

On days I bring only for myself, I'm named Break, but those days are few and far between.

The familiar jingle sounds as the doors swing open and closed, just as fast.

I repeat the same, every day routine and
Joey hands me my bag, my card, and a kind
look.

"It wasn't 2010, so I went somewhere else
and used it as credit," it was the same order,
same packaging, same smell, different
company symbol, and I was alright with
that.

But right then, when I couldn't put my
finger on the logo, totally unrecognizable by
either name or address, that's when I should
have been named Saint None.

I go to the back, I pull up a chair, I set up a

spot, I sit where I can see Jorge, small,

pixelated, black and white, Jorge.

I pull out a burger, unwrap the unfamiliarly

symbolized white wrapper and bite in;

warm, enveloping my tongue in flavors,

some unrecognizable, some as familiar as

my debit card pin number.

My soda isn't cold, it's flat, it's tasteless,

and it's in a plastic cup.

My fries have no shelter, no bag, and no salt.

I eat it all, I devour it, I choke down an

unrecognizable meal, and little Jeremy is

staring at the camera, helping a customer,

looking back, helping.

Now, I'm curious, am I named Gullible right

now?

Am I named Oblivious?

Jim has a name all set up and laid out for

me, but he can't tell me, he can't show me;

he's two inches tall and he's putting objects

and receipts in bags, one right after the

other.

His little, gray, beady eyes stare into mine when I feel the very first grumble, deep in my gut, right behind my belly button.

I scan the bag, it's not even a paper bag, it's a plastic bag; and then I realize that my phone never vibrated.

My back pocket never notified me of a debit card transaction.

My name is Gullible, as I fish my phone, shocked at the total lack of notification, total lack of addition going on within me, within my stomach, grumbling and churning what

I'd just swallowed, my flat soda with a

funny tasting burger and salt-less fries.

Break isn't over for another fifteen minutes,

company policy says.

Jason's two inch frame isn't even visible

anymore, he can't see me and I can't see

him, but I have the backroom keys and

Gullible is closest to the bathroom, company

policy says.

I try the whole, 'finger my uvula' to make

myself throw up, but my gut isn't telling me

which direction it wants to go, so I opt for a

seat on the ground.

I can laugh at the boy, I can laugh at him for coming in late, for being hired for the bottom, for gaining minimum wage, for having a kid and wife at home depending on him, I can laugh at everything he stands for, but I'm the one sitting on the bathroom floor, thirteen minutes until show time, company policy says.

My gut decides up, and I hold it in long enough to lean over, the breath knocked out me from doing just that much.

I lay on the toilet seat long enough to catch my breath, but it's cool against my sweating skin, cool against my new name, Skilled Sailor.

It just pours out in that moment, a current of multi-colored fluid hitting the transparent blue waters and snaking its way around the white porcelain and back to my cheeks, Newton's third law is the first thing I think about.

Its eleven minutes more of labored gulps of air and hooded eyes upon a rubber face, a rubber face that makes its way across the linoleum floor, to the mirror. Yeah, a white, rubber eraser, dotted with sweat and little light brown specs.

My gut then decides down and I don't make it, but I'm lying on my side and thinking about new names, thinking about when the new kid is going to realize that I'm not going back out there, or when he's going to let me in on what he's seeing from his black and white, pixelated side of the universe.

The second hand doesn't even hit nine more

minutes when my gut decides that it can no longer decide, and I'm dragging myself to the door, reaching for the fifty foot high handle.

I'm dragging a one hundred and twenty pound body who just shit itself, across the back room of a retailer, in the bathroom, and, oh, how little black and white Jack must feel about his accomplishments right now.

The pain is so immense that I can't even feel it, my gut just decided to stop working, it won't decide from either up or down, and it's the best feeling I've ever experienced.

I have the white gate opened and I flop down to the other side, my face sticking to the linoleum, looking for anything that can help me, and then my gut decides up, and there's a current of blood all around my head, grasping onto anything it can latch onto, like the desk holding the five by five TV, with little Jacob's face, staring back at me.

If I didn't know any better, if I could just

inch up to that little illuminated square, I could probably see his little smile, his little transparent lips, whispering different names for me.

But I don't see him, I don't inch up to the TV, I just lay there, shit in my pants and bloody vomit smeared over me, with my eyes closed, realizing the most perfect name for myself, Saint Free.

Saint Free of overdraft fees, since I had only two dollars to spend, Saint Free of embarrassment, now, Saint Free of little

Jaden's face.

I'm Saint Free and my story has ended.

Old man

Old man, old man

I heard you tried to get us to leave

I heard you coming on over

Because you couldn't believe it

Because you wanted to be it

We'd never cut off a corpse

We'd never sew up a heart

We'd never kill a good hombre

We'd never mess around

But we've got to go

Because we know that you know

That you've been a good hombre

And that you'd never make a sound